80-YEAR-OLD ELEPHANTS!

By Leonard Atlantic

Gareth Stevens
PUBLISHING

Please visit our website, www.garethstevens.com. For a free color catalog of all our high-quality books, call toll free 1-800-542-2595 or fax 1-877-542-2596.

Cataloging-in-Publication Data

Names: Atlantic, Leonard.
Title: 80-year-old elephants! / Leonard Atlantic.
Description: New York : Gareth Stevens Publishing, 2017. | Series: World's longest-living animals | Includes index.
Identifiers: ISBN 9781482456097 (pbk.) | ISBN 9781482456134 (library bound) | ISBN 9781482456127 (6 pack)
Subjects: LCSH: Elephants–Juvenile literature.
Classification: LCC QL737.P98 A43 2017 | DDC 599.67–dc23

Published in 2017 by
Gareth Stevens Publishing
111 East 14th Street, Suite 349
New York, NY 10003

Designer: Andrea Davison-Bartolotta and Bethany Perl
Editor: Ryan Nagelhout

Photo credits: Cover, p. 1 compuinfoto/iStock/Thinkstock.com; pp. 2–24 (background) Dmitrieva Olga/Shutterstock.com; p. 5 Toey Toey/Shutterstock.com; p. 7 (Asian elephant) Signature Message/Shutterstock.com; p. 7 (African elephant) john michael evan potter/Shutterstock.com; p. 9 (African elephant) Patryk Kosmider/Shutterstock.com; p. 9 (Asian elephant) Anan Kaewkhammul/Shutterstock.com; p. 11 Tish1/Shutterstock.com; p. 13 Claudia Paulussen/Shutterstock.com; p. 15 (clouds) detchana wangkheeree/Shutterstock.com; p. 15 (Lin Wang) Unknown/Wikipedia.org; p. 17 JAMES HUANG/Getty Images; p. 19 ullstein bild/Getty Images; p. 21 Joseph Sohm/Shutterstock.com.

Printed in the United States of America

CPSIA compliance information: Batch #CW17GS: For further information contact Gareth Stevens, New York, New York at 1-800-542-2595.

CONTENTS

Boldface words appear in the glossary.

Big and Old

Elephants are the largest land animals on Earth. They're also some of the longest living. These huge animals are **mammals** like humans. Some have even lived longer than the average human! Let's learn more about these amazing animals.

Asian or African

There are two main groups of elephants: Asian and African. African elephants are slightly larger than their Asian cousins. They also have bigger ears! African elephant ears are actually shaped a bit like the **continent** Africa.

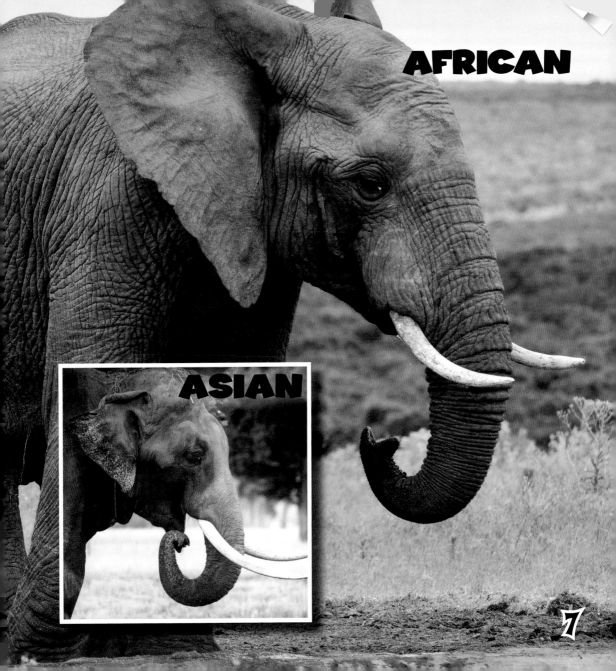

AFRICAN

ASIAN

Walking Tall

African elephants stand between 8.2 and 13 feet (2.5 and 4 m) tall! They can weigh between 2.5 and 7 tons (2.3 and 6.4 mt). Asian elephants are between 6.6 and 9.8 feet (2 and 3 m) tall and weigh between 2.25 and 5.5 tons (2 and 5 mt).

AFRICAN

ASIAN

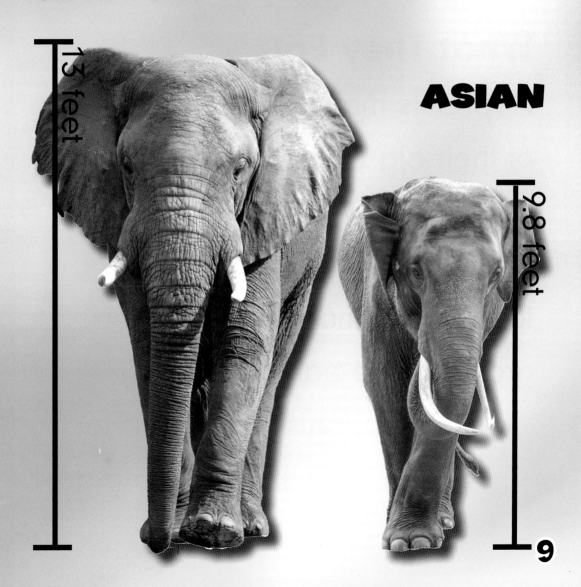

13 feet

9.8 feet

9

What They Eat

Elephants may look scary because of their big **tusks**, which are made of ivory. However, they only eat plants! They use their tusks for digging and eat mostly roots, grasses, tree bark, and fruit. African elephants can eat up to 300 pounds (136 kg) of food a day!

How Old?

In the wild, African elephants live up to 70 years and Asian elephants live up to 60 years. That's pretty awesome. But elephants in zoos can live to be 80 years old! Elephants are **pregnant** for 22 months before they have babies!

Lin Wang

Lin Wang was one of the oldest elephants ever studied. In 2003, he died in a zoo in Taiwan at age 86! Lin Wang lived an amazing life. He served in both the Japanese and Chinese armies during World War II!

After the war, Lin Wang was moved from Burma to China. He worked in a circus and in construction.

Lin Wang then moved from China to the Taiwan Zoo, where he became famous. For years, people visited him to celebrate his birthday!

Life in Zoos

Some people feel zoos keep elephants safe from poachers, or people who kill elephants for their ivory. Zoos say elephants live longer there. But some studies say zoos actually shorten the **lifespan** of some elephants because of disease, stress, or overeating.

Keeping Them Safe

Keeping elephants healthy so they can live long lives is hard work. Animal preserves try to give elephants lots of space to live and keep poachers away. Asian elephants are **endangered**, and African elephants are at risk of being endangered. They need our help to stay safe!

GLOSSARY

continent: one of the seven largest landmasses on Earth: Asia, Africa, North America, South America, Antarctica, Europe, and Australia

endangered: in danger of dying out

lifespan: the average length of time an animal lives

mammal: a warm-blooded animal that has a backbone and hair, breathes air, and feeds milk to its young

pregnant: expected to give birth

tusk: a very long tooth that sticks out of an animal's mouth

FOR MORE INFORMATION

BOOKS

Furstinger, Nancy. *African Elephants*. Mankato, MN:
The Child's World, 2016.

Hansen, Grace. *Elephants*. North Mankato, MN: ABDO Kids, 2016.

Marsico, Katie. *Elephants*. New York, NY: Children's Press, 2017.

WEBSITES

6 Amazing Animals That Practically Lived Forever
mentalfloss.com/article/29830/6-amazing-animals-practically-lived-forever
Read more about Lin Wang the elephant and other amazing animals here.

African Elephant
animals.nationalgeographic.com/animals/mammals/african-elephant/
Learn more about African elephants at this National Geographic site.

Asian Elephant
animals.nationalgeographic.com/animals/mammals/asian-elephant/
Find out more about Asian elephants and how they live here.

INDEX